STREAMS
THE FOURFOLD
INCOME STRATEGY

by
Josh Watters

STREAMS: THE FOURFOLD INCOME STRATEGY
JOSH WATTERS

Copyright © 2017 Watters & Company.

All Rights Reserved.

First Edition: December 2017
Printed in the United States of America
ISBN: 9781948339285

To order more copies for you or your team, go to WattersandCompany.com or contact Watters & Company at 614-342-0005.

To my wife and three lovely daughters -
Taylor, Laila, and Malia.
You all are my greatest inspiration.
I do it all for you!

Table of Contents

PREFACE

I was inspired to write this book after receiving an invite to share some wisdom and experience before a group of teenaged kids. One of my best friends, the organizer of the event, invited me to share stories of my success in entrepreneurship and to provide an engaging activity to get the kids interested in their finances. As I prepared my very short talk, I started to realize that it was going to be impossible to leave the lasting impression that I wanted in the limited amount of time that I would have with the students. I felt like more was required of me, because after all, I may never have another chance to leave my mark on their young and hungry minds.

Over the past few years, I have been getting invited to speak in the areas of entrepreneurship and finance more frequently, but I hadn't done the job of creating a book or a resource that I could leave with all who hear me speak. I needed a tangible product that would reinforce my most shared financial strategy on acquiring and maintaining wealth.

So I chose to write the book that I wish I had read before I became a wage-earning adult.

I'll apologize upfront for the lack of

sophistication that is presented in this book. I wrote this book in only a few hours. It was proofread and edited by my wife and small group of friends, self-published, and shipped. Needless to say, my emphasis was execution and speed to market.

I had to get this book out of me quickly, or risk never completing it.

This book was written to create successful, six and seven-figure earners. What I share in this book is exactly what I've done to grow my own income to a place beyond what most people would ever imagine possible.

This book holds the keys to creating four sustainable streams of income, using what is already inside of you.

So open your mind, have faith in your ability, and decide that from this day forward you will make the necessary change to produce a life of wealth for yourself, your family and your community.

Deuteronomy 8:18 - "But remember the LORD your God, for it is he who gives you the ability to produce wealth..."

2 Corinthians 9:11 "You will be enriched in every way so that you can be generous on every occasion, and through us your generosity will result in thanksgiving to God."

CHAPTER 1
THE PREFERRED
WAY TO WEALTH

Money, money, money. We work most of our lives to attain it. We always seem to need more, and yet there never seems to be enough.

When you were a kid did you think you would grow up and be rich? What about today - do you still believe that wealth is a possibility for you?

I'm talking about wealth beyond living from *"paycheck to paycheck"*.

Wealth that doesn't worry about being laid off.

Wealth that will be passed onto your children and their children.

True wealth starts with how you think

From childhood I knew that I wanted to earn more than enough money to one day take good care of my family. My father was always a good provider for our family, but we didn't consider ourselves wealthy. My mother stayed at home to raise my siblings and me. We regularly lived paycheck to paycheck. I can remember my father working two, sometimes three jobs just to make ends meet. While I was fortunate to have both of my parents in the home, we certainly had our fair share of financial stress. We never had the wealth we needed to live in financial peace. We never escaped the rat race of debt, lack and uncertainty.

These are the experiences that shape my perspective today. Today I live in financial abundance and peace. Not because I work multiple jobs or 80 hours each week. I live this way because I've created what I like to call *the preferred way to wealth*.

The common way to wealth

Think about this for a moment. For many adults, the path to building wealth goes as follows:

- Go to school from ages five through eighteen
- Go to college
- Find a job, maybe two
- Work 5 or more days every week until you can retire*

- If married, both spouses work outside of the home and live paycheck-to-paycheck
- Work past retirement because of financial instability
- Pass away leaving little to no wealth to your family

Note that this way of life will likely involve trading the most valuable and largest chunk of your life glued to a desk, missing your children grow up, or spending an unhealthy number of nights working 2nd and 3rd shift in a warehouse.

To be honest, this way of life isn't all bad. Americans have the opportunity to live better than the citizens of many other countries. This way of life can even be lived with some significantly good experiences. I know a lot of friends, family members and acquaintances who are living this way and consider this lifestyle a success. I do not judge or condemn anyone for this way of life, it's just contrary to the life I choose to live. And if you are reading this book, it's probably not the life you want for yourself either.

I would like to suggest to you that there is a better way to live.

The preferred way to wealth

The preferred way to wealth is reaching financial stability without compromising the things you value most in life. The preferred way to wealth has your passions, your skills, beliefs and purpose at the core.

The preferred way to wealth must be created by investing in yourself, then giving your best to the people who need you the most -- in business, on the job, and in your networks.

The preferred way to wealth involves building four streams of income.

The preferred way to wealth values stability and the experiences found in your journey to wealth over greed and get-rich-quick schemes.

Finally, the preferred way to wealth is rooted in gratitude and generosity. Gratitude to the Creator for the gifts that you possess, and the ability to serve people. And generosity -- giving when there is need, and helping others along the way.

Imagine living a rich life. Not just riches like having millions of dollars in the bank. There are a lot of miserable millionaires who I wouldn't consider to live a rich life.

When I say "rich life", I speak of a life rich in experiences: meaningful relationships, the freedom to travel, people and cultures to discover, and fine cuisine to savor. A life of freedom and liberation. A life with the power to make decisions not dictated by your work schedule or punching the time clock at the workplace. A life of community, pouring into the lives of others, teaching what you know and adding value to the world with your words, your actions, your art, and your experiences.

This rich lifestyle is typically only attainable to those with the financial means to live it.

Would you believe that there are some people just like you and I who actually do what they love for a living and get paid to do it?

Although uncommon, this way of life is not a fantasy. It is a very true reality for a lot of people who use their God given talents, skills and natural abilities to *create* their success. In fact, I have been living this way for the past few years of my life (once it finally "clicked" for me). This book's intention is to help you on your path to this new way of life.

* Did you know?: From age 22-65, over 500 months of your life will be spent working a job or building your career.

Wouldn't it be nice to **truly live** during these years? Don't wake up one day in your 60's with regret -- wishing you would've tried that business idea, made that career move, or pursued that dream of yours.

There is a better way to create wealth, and those who have attained it know that it starts with how you think.

Proverbs 20:5 "The purposes of a person's heart are deep waters, but one who has insight draws them out."

CHAPTER 2
WHAT IS YOUR FREEDOM WORTH?

Money is what binds us, stresses us, and controls many of the decisions we make in life. It can also be what liberates us, provides for our needs, gives us influence, and allows us to generously aid our friends, families, and communities.

Who do you believe is responsible for ensuring that you live a rich life during your limited time on this earth? Is it up to your employer? Was it your parents' responsibility?

There are career fairs full of people looking for jobs. Some because they are unemployed, some seeking to earn more, and yet others in search of a more fulfilling existence.

What if I were to tell you that all of your wealth begins with you. The answer is inside of you. No one can care or do more to ensure your success than you. Everyone has *something* that they are good at. Everyone has a natural gifting or inclination that must be nurtured or acted upon to live an abundant, fulfilling life.

Your wealth is inside of you.

The story of the "Golden Voice" Ted Williams

I'd like to share the story of a once-homeless man from my city. The man's name is Ted Williams, and he has a god-given "Golden Voice". Ted Williams, an older man, had struggled with drug addiction and homelessness. Without getting too much into his personal life story, I'll skip to the part where he used what he had within to bring forth abundance.

Standing on the street with a sign that read "I have a God given gift of voice", he was discovered by a local journalist who video-recorded his interaction with Mr. Williams.

To make a long story short, the video was posted online and it quickly went viral. Williams has since done voice work with radio stations, the NFL, Pepsi, Kraft, and others. When he chose to share his gift with the world, he was given another chance at life.

You see, Mr. Williams had the ability to produce wealth inside of him all along. And thanks to his viral video, he has amassed a compassionate audience who actually wants to see him succeed. He will likely never go hungry again. Ted Williams' life has renewed purpose.

Similar to most things in life, building wealth is most rewarding (and typically easier) when you use your natural gifts, and when you can be true to yourself. This is why it is important to look within yourself when exploring what it is that you will do to create a new level of wealth for your life.

So who are you really? What comes easy to you, but other people seem to struggle with?

Leveraging your best talents and your most unique gifts are what will not only set you apart, but also set you up to prosper in life. In order to do this, you'll have to dig deep down inside of yourself. You'll also have to put fear, doubt, shame, guilt, and unworthiness out of your life. It takes some vulnerability to share what you believe is your gift with the world.

But the risk is usually worth the reward.

Every time I meet with a new client I risk rejection. Each time I teach a workshop or speak to a new group of people, I have to battle the doubt and fear of failure that comes along with it. Conversely, each time I get a "yes" from a client or that standing ovation after sharing my voice, I realize just how much the risk is worth.

It should encourage you to know that every successful person has faced the same risks, fears and emotions. We're all human.

So ask yourself this: How much is your financial freedom worth? Is it worth taking risks and making yourself vulnerable to friends, family, customers and clients? Then decide that your freedom and wealth is worth more than your fears, and more than the opinions of others.

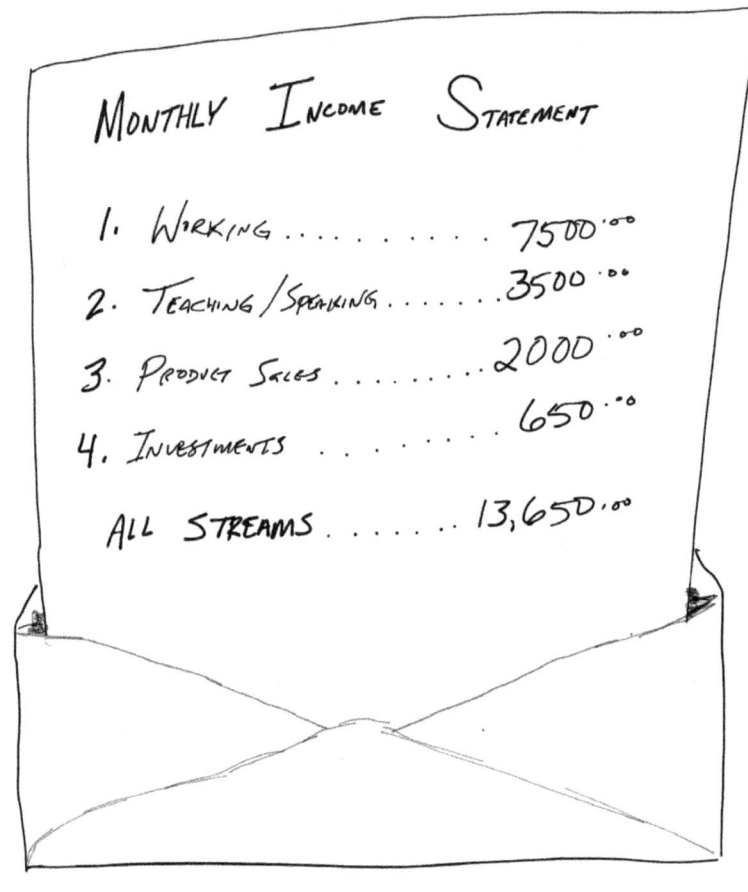

Genesis 2:10 "A river watering the garden flowed from Eden; from there it was separated into four headwaters."

CHAPTER 3
YOUR FOUR STREAMS

If you lost your primary stream of income today (your job, your business, etc), how would you earn a living? What would be your backup plan?

Right out of college, I worked a part-time internship while freelancing as a web developer. I knew that there was always the threat of the internship contract ending, so it was important to me that I began growing another stream of income as I was just beginning to understand that being an adult basically just meant paying rent, bills, and student loans.

It wasn't long into my career before people started to take notice to my skills as a web developer and technologist. I stood out a bit because not many young black men were into Information Technology at the time. Before I knew it I was being asked to do all kinds of odd jobs -- build websites, fix computers, teaching computer literacy to the elderly. I somehow even found myself doing taxes! People were literally throwing potentially new streams of income at me. But they weren't sustainable, and I was spreading myself too thin.

I was enjoying the extra checks and cash each month, outside of my internship but I knew there had to be a more sustainable, coordinated way to grow meaningful streams of income.

Surety and stability come from having multiple income streams.

Think about some of the most spectacular and stable structures in the world. The Eiffel Tower, skyscrapers, pyramids, etc. Most of their strength comes from their base of fours. Four sides, points and positions create some of the most stable structures in the world -- The Eiffel Tower's four legs, four sided skyscrapers and buildings, four cornered pyramids and four tires on cars.

Of course in some cases, more sides or legs could prove even more stable, but four seems to be the most effective without compromising efficiency. More sides, legs, tires and corners also means more attention and maintenance.

My theory is that in order to live a life of wealth and abundance without risking overkill, stress, and exhaustion, you'll have to learn to create and master four streams of income.

Think about the idea of building four income streams. You'll start to notice a pattern in people who have mastered stream-building.

Let's look at some examples:

Professional athletes typically earn their dollar based on their athletic ability. Much work goes into playing at a professional level and earning above average wages. Ambitious, top-tier athletes use their offseason building their audience through teaching and training at camps. A number of top-tier athletes even turn their success into endorsements, or create their own line of products and gear. A lesser known stream comes from their investments: restaurants, car lots, movie theatres, and the like.

Of course, some athletes only get paid for playing their sport, trading their time for dollars.

Which type of athlete is your current income most similar to?

Celebrities grow their audience because of their great talent, charisma, and/or art. Their success often catapults into fan clubs, book deals, products, and more. It is also common to see celebrities start or support nonprofit or charity organizations and foundations.

Many **motivational speakers** gain popularity because they have already exhibited success in an area of their lives, be it family, business, etc. Their streams usually include teaching and selling products like books and videos of their best work.

Pastors and ministers are mastering the four streams as well. When not preaching to their congregation, many pastors are penning books, teaching workshops, speaking at conferences, or buying up property in their area.

Entrepreneurs of businesses, both big and small, are quickly rising as masters of the four streams model as well. They perform services day-to-day for some clients, while teaching and selling products to other clients.

Everyday people are working their day jobs and moonlighting as bakers, musicians, artists, hair stylists, teachers, handymen, and more.

Are these examples of multi-stream earners getting you excited to start building streams of your own?

My "aha!" moment

The example that brought it all home for me were the countless business owners turned bloggers who had mastered their four streams. A few years ago I began following a number of bloggers who were in the tech sector just like me. They were often freelancers or had started their own small firms. Through their writing, these average, everyday people were growing audiences who looked to them as mentors. These bloggers then began releasing products: eBooks, apps, and other products - to which their loyal fans and audiences were eager to buy (myself included).

Through their example, I learned that I too could become this type of entrepreneur. I had to use my most valuable skills to strategically create these streams of income.

Earn with the work of your hands. Teach what you know. Create products. Invest your wealth.

Work. Teach. Create. Invest.

Once I began thinking in terms of streams, everything changed. I knew that if I could master these streams, I would never have to worry about money again.

Financial drought, lack, and scarcity cannot easily quench four flowing streams.

THE WORK
OF YOUR

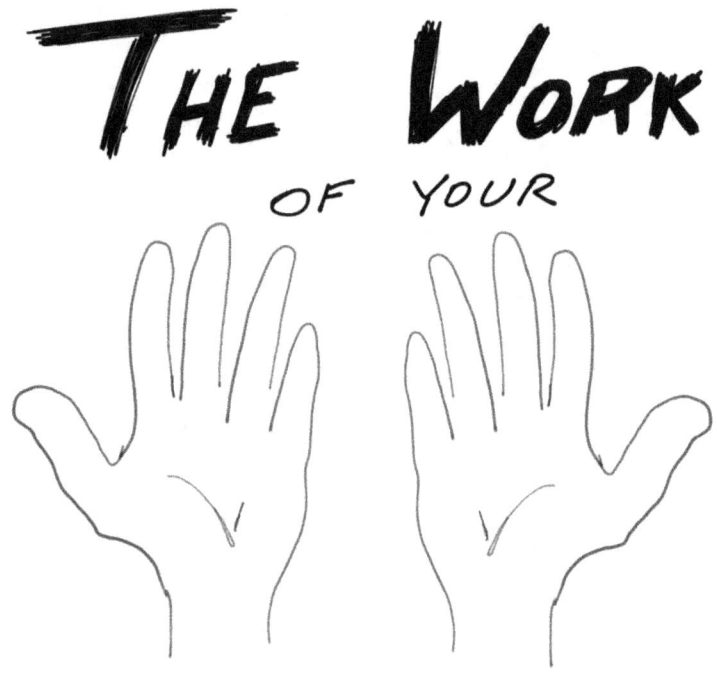

Deuteronomy 28:12 "The LORD will open the heavens, the storehouse of his bounty, to send rain on your land in season and to bless all the work of your hands."

CHAPTER 4
THE **WORK**
OF YOUR HANDS

Your first step towards wealth actually begins with putting in the work. This part is usually inescapable. Anything worth having will take some work to attain. This is the time to grind and sweat it out to earn your early dollars. Dollars that when used strategically, will help you create your future streams.

I call this the work of your hands. It's not always glamorous. The work of your hands is about using what you have to generate income.

The work of your hands is usually a trading of your services for dollars. Your service typically involves the combination of mind, body and time -- three of the most important and most limited assets we have as human beings.

The work of your hands is what makes you valuable to others, day to day. Your employer needs your mind, body and time to best serve and build the corporation. As a business owner, your client/customers need your mind, body and time to serve them.

In exchange for your mind, body and time you collect checks and earn your wages, usually just enough to live a life reliant on financing and in debt to creditors. In other words, living paycheck to paycheck.

Whether you work a day job or operate your own business, your main source of income is likely earned by the work of your hands.

For most, it's just too big a risk to do full-time self employment or to drop everything and start a business. Others will keep their full time job and moonlight their skills to earn on the side. A daring few will take the risk and start the business that they know is inside of them, just waiting to be released to the world.

Below are examples of common first stream businesses. I will build upon this table through the next couple of chapters to help generate ideas for a variety of fields:

Stream #1 - WORK	Stream #2 - TEACH	Stream #3 - CREATE
Building Websites		
Baking Cakes		
Graphic Design		
Auto Repair		
Musician		
Social Media		
Marketing		
Copywriting		
Physical Training		
Hair Stylist/Barber		
Fashion Stylist		
Dietician		

These are just examples. Don't be afraid to think outside of the box!

You do this every day. You must be an expert!

Your first stream of income will also help you to gain credibility in your field. If employed, ideally you work in a field that you are passionate about. If not it may be time to start looking to earn a living elsewhere. If you've started your own business, you are likely already positioning yourself as an expert and just need to build a portfolio and a track record success. Perform your first stream of income with excellence and it will propel you towards your next streams of income.

The goal here is to build one stable and profitable stream that can begin to fund your other streams.

Proverbs 11:25 "A generous person will prosper; whoever refreshes others will be refreshed."

CHAPTER 5
TEACH WHAT YOU KNOW

When following my guide to building income streams, timing the birth of your streams is important. It is important that you dominate the work of your hands before moving onto your second stream. Each additional stream's viability is greatly enhanced by the success of the previous stream.

All of the training and education you've received up to this point in your life has helped you earn a living in your field, on your job, or in your business. So to whom do you owe your success? Who taught you how to fine-tune your craft, how to focus your efforts, and how to continue getting better at what you do? Past teachers, mentors, professors, coaches or trainers were certainly involved at some point.

I think you're starting to get where I'm going with this. You've made it to where you are today because others taught you what you know.

Thinking back, what are some of the lessons and strategies that you really needed to know in order to become your best? Would you have been willing to pay to learn the things that earn you the most money?

People pay for workshops and learning opportunities all the time.

Now is the time to put the teaching shoes on your feet, because this is where your second stream of income will manifest. It's time to pay it forward. It's time for you to teach others what you know.

There is great value in teaching what you know

As I grew my business over the years, there were a handful of people I listened to and learned from. People like Nathan Barry (founder of ConvertKit), who always worked and experimented in public, sharing successes and shortcomings along the way. Nathan had a story and skill set very similar to my own, and I enjoyed learning from him as he tried new ways to grow his income. I was always more interested in following the "average Joe's" who had found success, as opposed to the CEO's of Fortune 500 companies.

What I hadn't realized is that thousands of miles away (Nathan is from Boise, Idaho), and despite the fact that he had never met me or even remotely known me, Nathan had become my mentor. Nathan was teaching me everything he knew.

It wasn't until Nathan wrote a blog post and created T-shirts with the phrase "Teach Everything You Know" that I came to this realization. He had me. I was more than just a subscriber to his email list. I had become a student and consumer of his method of teaching. I've purchased his products, read his blog posts and listened to his podcast.

While at one point I felt like we were growing together, it was obvious that Nathan Barry had become an authority to not only me but thousands of others worldwide.

This is the value of teaching what you know. You become a trusted authority.

Somebody needs what you have

One evening, a friend and I were brainstorming areas we felt qualified to teach. We remembered being at a place early in our professional journeys where we had no identifiable mentors or resources to teach us some of the things we wanted to know most.

All of a sudden it hit me.

Every year there are new high schoolers, college students and business owners that are just as clueless as we once were.

This idea goes even further than that. Every day, someone is venturing into starting a business, leaving their job, starting a new hobby, playing a new sport, learning a new instrument, etc. Here is where your opportunity exists.

Humans rely on one another for teaching and learning.

But do you qualify?

Have you ever had to show someone how to do something? Anything? Then it's just that simple: Yes, I believe you qualify to teach.

I'll add onto the stream table to provide ideas for teaching opportunities:

Stream #1 - WORK	Stream #2 - TEACH	Stream #3 - CREATE
Building Websites	Teach a workshop	
Baking Cakes	Cook on Youtube	
Graphic Design	Teach a class	
Auto Repair	Teach your neighbors	
Musician	Teach playing lessons	
Social Media	Host a webinar	
Marketing	Teach a workshop	
Copywriting	Teach a workshop	
Physical Training	Coach	
Hair Stylist/Barber	Teach grooming	
Fashion Stylist	Teach style tips	
Dietician	Teach healthy habits	

Start small. Teach on your job. Teach to your neighbors. Teach in your community. Teach new techniques that make you more productive. Teach others "your way" of doing things. Teach via Skype, Google Hangouts or social media. Host a free class first, and then offer a paid follow-up class. It won't be long before you find opportunities to monetize your ability to teach, but you may be responsible for creating the opportunities.

Grow to the place where your paid teaching happens regularly and *voila!* -- teaching has become your second stream of income.

Galatians 6:9 "And let us not grow weary of doing good, for in due season we will reap, if we do not give up."

CHAPTER 6
CREATE YOUR PRODUCT

I finally did it. Creating this book completes a huge milestone on my life's bucket list. This book is the first written product I have released into the marketplace. It is the first of many written products that I intend to release.

But I didn't become an author because I have a love or passion for writing. To be quite honest, writing was never something I saw as a strength or passion of mine. Instead, I see immense value in creating *products* -- whether that product is a book or not doesn't really matter.

Look at it this way: most of what I am sharing in this book, I share with people around me almost daily in regular conversation. I've even taught some of these principles in small groups and workshops, but I cannot be everywhere at once. This book gives me the opportunity to share a piece of myself with the world in an instant. That is valuable. Multiplying your reach is important.

So now it's time for you to get creative! The product you create has the ability to become scalable, repeatable, and perhaps most importantly, *passive*.

A passive stream of income is a good stream of income since you will likely already be busy with working and teaching your other streams. First, let's look at the greatest benefits of creating a product and then we'll decide what product you should create.

Creating product income buys back your time and multiplies your reach.

Yes, you read that right. The third stream of income will actually help you begin to free up your time. The nature of products is that once created, it can be sold over and over again with little to no ongoing labor. This gives you the power to increase your wealth exponentially.

Think about this: if given the opportunity could you...

- Individually teach one person from every city in America in a day's time? **No, but your book or online course could.**
- Create custom birthday party decor for twenty different birthday parties this weekend? **No, but you could probably sell twenty premade decor packages online.**
- Do 1-on-1 fitness and health training with

100 different people daily? **No, but your workout videos and nutrition plans could.**

Are you starting to understand how product creation can buy back your time? Build it right once and your product can earn for you, while still serving your customers. Before you know it, you will be making money in your sleep.

Literally.

Many people who sell products online wake up more rich than when they went to sleep because ecommerce doesn't stop when you "clock out". Every dollar that you begin to make from your product is no longer connected to your time. Yes it will take time and energy to create, but eventually this stream can become completely passive.

Create a product that comes naturally

Maybe you are still wondering "How can I possibly add another stream? Where will I find the time?"

To these questions, my answer is this: *create a product that comes naturally.*

If you are struggling to find time to conceptualize or develop a product, why not do something that comes naturally from one of your previous streams? Build a *byproduct*. This book is a byproduct of the teaching/speaking I do as an entrepreneur. I share my story and the strategies found in this book to kids, adults, and other aspiring entrepreneurs. The difference is that this book can go places that I cannot physically go. As stated earlier, it *multiplies my reach* and *frees my time*.

Some of my other products are more discreet, but still byproducts. For instance, I've created training products that I offer to clients of my web marketing firm.

Whatever product you decide to create, it must be accessible, scalable, and easy to replicate and sell globally. This is the way to begin earning money while you sleep or while vacationing, enjoying your favorite hobbies, or building your other streams.

Still haven't settled on what to make your product stream? Let's go back to the stream chart to help you generate some ideas:

Stream #1 - WORK	Stream #2 - TEACH	Stream #3 - CREATE
Building Websites	Teach a workshop	Create web themes
Baking Cakes	Cook on Youtube	Create a cookbook
Graphic Design	Teach a class	Design T-shirts, fonts
Auto Repair	Teach your neighbors	Create how-to videos
Musician	Teach playing lessons	Produce an album
Social Media	Host a webinar	Write an ebook
Marketing	Teach a workshop	Write an ebook
Copywriting	Teach a workshop	Write an ebook
Physical Training	Coach	Create a workout plan
Hair Stylist/Barber	Teach grooming	Create a product
Fashion Stylist	Teach style tips	Create a fashion item
Dietician	Teach healthy habits	Create a diet plan

Releasing a product created from within you will be more than worth it. And not just from a financial perspective. Doing what it takes to say that you created a book, an album, a software, a course, or any other type of product takes a lot of courage and puts you into a class of creatives, builders and inventors. Your product also helps position you as an authority in your field. How many people do you know that can say they've written and released a book? Or how about an album? Probably not many. Now think of those who *have* authored a book or released an album. Those are the doers. Be like those people.

I must add that this income stream is typically the toughest stream to execute and launch. It's like an added bit of vulnerability to actually package something and release it as your own. Fear of opinions and fear of failure have to be set aside because as soon as you get past those, your product has the chance to become one of your most liberating streams of income.

Ecclesiastes 11:3 "Invest in seven ventures, yes, in eight; you do not know what disaster may come upon the land."

CHAPTER 7
INVEST NOW,
EARN FOREVER

Finally ready to take on your final stream of income?

Before even thinking about jumping into investing, it is important to note that there is plenty of risk associated with building this stream -- risk that the average, single income earning person typically isn't willing to take on. But for you, investing can be a more realistic and pursuable stream of income (since you have set up at least three other proven streams of income, right?).

There are many ways to invest. Business ventures, real estate, and the stock market are some of the more common options. Once you reach the point when you are financially ready to invest, you'll have plenty options to choose from. Regardless of what other sources suggest, building wealth through investments is a decision that should come after thorough personal research. It will be important for you to understand the surety and risks of each. It will also be beneficial to choose a style of investing that fits you and your lifestyle best.

My advice: invest in yourself first. Only test the waters of traditional investing after you've invested in yourself, your business, your teaching and your products. Sometimes reinvesting into what you already have is enough to earn more substantially more in your streams. Try investing to better market your current business and products. Also invest in conferences and educational opportunities for yourself.

But let's shift gears to more traditional investing.

The best investments are those that pay you back regularly -- like monthly checks from rental property, or profits from business venture income. These are my favorite types of investments, but if they don't immediately appeal to you, keep reading.

When choosing a mode of investment that best fits your lifestyle, it is important to choose investments that won't throw your other streams off balance. For instance, while actively growing your other streams of income, it would make sense to choose an investment that doesn't require much of your personal time or energy: stocks, mutual funds, money markets, or certificate of deposits (google the term "compound interest"). Or, if you are at a place in life where your other income streams are more hands-off, it might make sense to get into more aggressive investments, like real estate or investing in a business venture.

The truth of the matter is that researching and maintaining investment streams can be just as time-consuming as your other streams. My preferred investment style is very low contact. I like the idea of throwing my money into something I believe in, and watching it grow over time. However, I am interested in becoming a more active investor when I no longer spend as much time in my working in my business and teaching.

James 2:17 "...faith by itself, if it is not accompanied by action, is dead."

CHAPTER 8
TAKE ACTION

So this is it -- you have nearly completed the book. You've got the game plan, but you're wondering "what's next?"

Maybe you've read up to this point and have come up with your own personal stream strategy (it may be vastly different than mine). The essential key is that you simply start.

It's go time, so let's do a final review to get you motivated.

Work.

Do your best work right where you are at. Start today. Be a great employee to your company and your boss. Look for areas to improve, innovate, or educate others. This is your first stream of income, so you'll want to do it well and use it as the springboard for what is to come.

Teach.

Find somewhere to teach or speak regularly. It

doesn't necessarily matter if what you teach has anything to do with what you are most passionate about at first, it only matters that you begin to speak. As you grow more comfortable, look for ways for your speaking to pay off.

Create an opportunity for yourself by hosting a workshop or training at your job, a local church, recreation center, library or coffee shop. If you're more into motivational speaking, go back to your high school or college and offer to speak to a group of students. Promote your engagement for free via social media to your friends and family.

Document your engagements via photo, video and/or audio. It will add credibility for landing future engagements, as well as encourage and motivate you to continue! In order for your teaching to become an actual income stream, you will have to market yourself well or create opportunities that occur regularly -- whether weekly or monthly.

Create.

Decide what will be your first product. A book? An online course? Maybe you'll sell fancy baked goods every weekend.

Whatever you decide to build, build it with intent to sell over and over again. Remember, we are building streams, not drips. Keep in mind that your product works best if it is *symbiotic* (mutually beneficial) to your other streams. Your work can promote your teaching; your teaching can promote your products; and so on.

Challenge yourself. You have more power than you think.

Invest.

Find a place to invest your money. The best investments are the ones that will pay you regularly (like an actual stream). Look for opportunities to create rental income, venture business income, and the like. If nothing else, find somewhere to park your extra money - like taking advantage of compounding interest and growth over time.

Investing in external ventures will likely come after you've invested plenty internally -- on yourself, your business and your product.

Just Start

Having each of the four streams going is great, but having even two streams is better than one. Just start somewhere.

And leave no room for excuse. Don't worry about whether or not you have the time.

Make time.

People make time for what is really important in life. How important is your financial success and stability? What can you adjust in your life today to begin your path to freedom through income streams?

There is a life full of opportunity awaiting you on the other side of wealth and financial stability. The world is eagerly waiting for you to unleash what is already inside of you. But you don't have to take on the whole world. Build an audience one person at a time.

You will need your audience of real people -- loyal followers. It is *people* who you will work with, teach, and create products for. People are who will finance your income streams - and you will see that it pays to be in the people business.